Grammar and punctuation
Workbook

Ages 8–9

Grammar and punctuation

Book End, Range Road, Witney, Oxfordshire, OX29 0YD
www.scholastic.co.uk

© 2015, Scholastic Ltd

1 2 3 4 5 6 7 8 9   5 6 7 8 9 0 1 2 3 4

British Library Cataloguing-in-Publication Data
A catalogue record for this book is available from the British Library.

ISBN 978-1407-14072-8
Printed by Ashford Colour Press

Editorial
Rachel Morgan, Jenny Wilcox, Tracy Kewley, Red Door Media

Design
Neil Salt, Nicolle Thomas

Cover Design
Nicolle Thomas

Illustration
Simon Walmesley

Cover Illustration
Eddie Rego

Contents

How to use this book

- *Scholastic English Skills Workbooks* help your child to practise and improve their skills in English.

- The content is divided into topics. Find out what your child is doing in school and dip into the practice activities as required.

- Keep the working time short and come back to an activity if your child finds it too difficult. Ask your child to note any areas of difficulty. Don't worry if your child does not 'get' a concept first time, as children learn at different rates and content is likely to be covered at different times throughout the school year.

- Check your child's answers at www.scholastic.co.uk/ses/grammar.

- Give lots of encouragement, complete the 'How did you do' for each activity and the progress chart as your child finishes each chapter.

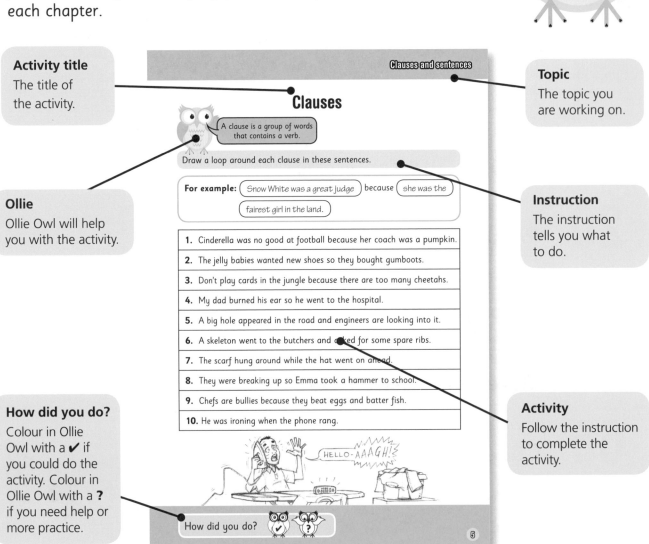

Activity title
The title of the activity.

Ollie
Ollie Owl will help you with the activity.

How did you do?
Colour in Ollie Owl with a ✔ if you could do the activity. Colour in Ollie Owl with a ? if you need help or more practice.

Topic
The topic you are working on.

Instruction
The instruction tells you what to do.

Activity
Follow the instruction to complete the activity.

Clauses

A clause is a group of words that contains a verb.

Draw a loop around each clause in these sentences.

For example: (Snow White was a great judge) because (she was the fairest girl in the land.)

1. Cinderella was no good at football because her coach was a pumpkin.
2. The jelly babies wanted new shoes so they bought gumboots.
3. Don't play cards in the jungle because there are too many cheetahs.
4. My dad burned his ear so he went to the hospital.
5. A big hole appeared in the road and engineers are looking into it.
6. A skeleton went to the butchers and asked for some spare ribs.
7. The scarf hung around while the hat went on ahead.
8. They were breaking up so Emma took a hammer to school.
9. Chefs are bullies because they beat eggs and batter fish.
10. He was ironing when the phone rang.

HELLO-AAAGH!

How did you do?

If you need help, ask an adult!

Clauses

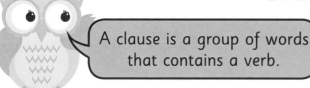

A clause is a group of words that contains a verb.

Draw a loop around each clause in these sentences.

For example: (Snow White was a great judge) because (she was the fairest girl in the land.)

1.	Cinderella was no good at football because her coach was a pumpkin.
2.	The jelly babies wanted new shoes so they bought gumboots.
3.	Don't play cards in the jungle because there are too many cheetahs.
4.	My dad burned his ear so he went to the hospital.
5.	A big hole appeared in the road and engineers are looking into it.
6.	A skeleton went to the butchers and asked for some spare ribs.
7.	The scarf hung around while the hat went on ahead.
8.	They were breaking up so Emma took a hammer to school.
9.	Chefs are bullies because they beat eggs and batter fish.
10.	He was ironing when the phone rang.

HELLO-AAAGH!

How did you do?

The clause bank

Complete each sentence with a clause from the clause bank.

Clause bank

a flying broomstick is a witchcraft   he didn't see the point

they did good turns all day   he told us a tall story

he had nobody to go with   his sister had told him a human story

1. The scouts got dizzy after _____

_____.

2. A plane is an aircraft, so _____

_____.

3. Jack couldn't do decimals as _____

_____.

4. The little ghost couldn't sleep because _____

_____.

5. A giant came to school and _____

_____.

6. The skeleton wanted to go to the disco but _____

_____.

How did you do?

Clause addition

Each clause must have a verb.

Add clauses to make longer sentences. The number in brackets shows how many clauses to add.

For example: A bat has wings. (3)
A bat has wings but it **is** a mammal because it **is** warm-blooded and **feeds** its young on milk.

1. A giraffe has a long neck _____. (1)

2. Postage stamps are sticky _____. (1)

3. Mr Singh went to the shops _____

_____. (2)

4. In our class 16 children walk to school _____

_____. (2)

5. We got lost in the maze _____

_____. (2)

6. My dad couldn't find his glasses _____

_____

_____. (3)

7. Yesterday we went swimming _____

_____

_____. (3)

How did you do?

Main or subordinate?

A main clause makes sense on its own but subordinate clause doesn't.

Underline the clauses in each notice. Highlight the main clauses in one colour and the subordinate clauses in another.

Watch found!

Come to the office if you have lost a watch.

Aikido Club

The Aikido Club welcomes new members since there is a special class for beginners.

Say 'Yes' to homework

Homework takes up your evenings although it helps in the long run.

Jim Goodwright's talk about homework is on Tuesday at 6pm. Get your homework done before coming along to the village hall.

Raffle

Win a prize!

Class 4 will be selling raffle tickets so that we can raise money for Children in Need.

Lost coat

Osman lost his coat on Friday afternoon. Can you help? Please check your coats so that you can let Osman know if you have it.

Litterbugs

Some people in our school don't use the bins, even though there are six of them. Please put your rubbish in a bin. If the bins are full, tell a teacher.

How did you do?

Conjunction connection

> A conjunction is a joining word

Join the clauses with conjunctions from the box.
Then use a different conjunction to change the meaning.

after	as	before	or
when	although	because	but
unless	and	in order that	if
until	then	so	so that

For example:

We won't go for a walk **because** it's raining.

We won't go for a walk **unless** it's raining.

1. I eat apples _____ they are red.

I eat apples _____ they are red.

2. We play football _____ it is cold.

We play football _____ it is cold.

3. My mum never buys fish _____ it is from the sea.

My mum never buys fish _____ it is from the sea.

4. You can play computer games _____ you can read.

You can play computer games _____ you can read.

5. The gate opens _____ the car passes the beam.

The gate opens _____ the car passes the beam.

How did you do?

Conjunction links

Choose a clause and a conjunction to complete each sentence. Underline each clause. Circle the conjunction.

Clauses	Conjunctions	
it never stopped raining	after	in case
I'm afraid of heights	and	or
he left the house	as	since
the clock struck midnight	as soon as	so
I can afford it	because	so that
the band played	before	unless
she broke her leg	but	until
it was scary	even though	when
you have a ticket	if	whenever

1. She has not played tennis _____.

2. The choir sang _____.

3. I enjoyed the film _____.

4. I never climb ladders _____.

5. He locked the door _____.

6. You can't get into the stadium _____.

7. We had a great holiday _____.

8. She stayed out _____.

9. I'll buy a new computer _____.

How did you do?

Lost clauses

Complete each sentence with its lost clause. Add a conjunction to join the clauses. Circle the conjunction.

not heard	they hatch	eat it
you can't make it drink	the cat's away	the horse has bolted
silence is golden	I'll scratch yours	the sun shines
	the pounds will look after themselves	

1. The mice will play _____.

2. Make hay _____.

3. You scratch my back _____.

4. You can't have your cake _____.

5. Don't count your chickens _____.

6. Don't shut the stable door _____.

7. You can take a horse to water _____.

8. Look after the pennies _____.

9. Speech is silver _____.

10. Children should be seen _____.

How did you do?

Use a conjunction

Write a clause before the conjunction.

Add another clause after the conjunction, to make a sentence.

For example:
The witch learned a new spell **so that** she could turn mud into ice cream.

1. _____ and _____.

2. _____ but _____.

3. _____ or _____.

4. _____ because _____.

5. _____ after _____.

6. _____ until _____.

7. _____ whenever _____.

8. _____ unless _____.

9. _____ before _____.

10. _____ after _____.

11. _____ so that _____.

12. _____ in case _____.

How did you do?

Adding information

Use a conjunction to add a clause to each sentence.

The sentence should answer the question.

Useful conjunctions for answering questions
Why? Why not? – because (reason), in case (possibility)
What for? – so, so that, in order to
When? – after, as, as soon as, before, since, until, when, whenever

1. The farmer crossed his sheep with porcupines

_____

_____ .

2. The opera singer climbed to the top of the ladder

_____

_____ .

3. The sausage rolled

_____

_____ .

4. It's very difficult to chat to a goat

_____

_____ .

How did you do?

Conjunctions in the gaps

Fill in the gaps in this passage with conjunctions to join the clauses.

Mr Crumble walked to the next village to see his friends, Mr and Mrs Wise.

He enjoyed the walk _____ it began to rain heavily. He had gone

too far to turn back _____ he kept on walking. He arrived at Mr and

Mrs Wise's house _____ a thunderstorm began.

Mr Wise opened the door _____ said, "It's lovely to see you

_____ you're soaked. Why didn't you bring an umbrella?"

"I left it on the bus _____ I went shopping last week," he replied.

Mr Wise brought some dry clothes _____ Mr Crumble could change.

The three friends enjoyed a hot meal _____ Mr Crumble thanked

them _____ said it was time to go. However, it was still raining

heavily _____ Mr Crumble's friends invited him to stay the night.

They showed him to his bedroom _____ went to bed. An hour later

the doorbell rang _____ they opened the door. It was

Mr Crumble, soaked to the skin.

They asked him where he had been

_____ he replied that he didn't

have his pyjamas with him _____

he had been home to get them!

How did you do?

Conjunctions in a story

Here's an idea. You could make up a story about someone who forgets to take their glasses when they go shopping. Imagine the mistakes they might make!

Write a short story, using conjunctions to join clauses in the sentences.

after	although	and	as	as if
as soon as	because	before	but	even if
even though	if	in case	now that	once
or	so	so that	then	unless
until	when	whenever	whereas	while

How did you do?

Sentence starters

Add a clause to each sentence, using a conjunction that helps to give information to answer the question. The sentences are in pairs.

1a. The homeless man spread out his sleeping bag

_____.

1b. He spread a big piece of plastic over the sleeping bag

_____.

2a. Mum never goes out without an umbrella

_____.

2b. She wears a thick, padded coat

_____.

3a. Bring something interesting to school tomorrow

_____.

3b. I'm going to keep my interesting object in a big sack

_____.

4a. If you find something you could take it to a police station

_____.

4b. If you lose something you could report it to the police

_____.

How did you do?

Sentence builders

Add two extra clauses to each sentence. Use conjunctions to add new clauses.

although	and	because	but
even though	if	so	so that
unless	when	whenever	

1. The man smashed the window _____

_____ .

Say what he did next and why.

2. James said he might help his mum in the garden

_____ .

Say what might make him help her and why.

3. Mrs Patel gives money to charities _____

_____ .

Say why this is very generous and what makes her do it.

4. My sister never wears a dress _____

_____ .

Add two activities she does that might make her wear a dress.

5. Jill put on a wetsuit _____

_____ .

Say what she put on the wetsuit for and why this was a strange thing to do.

How did you do?

A passage of long sentences

Ellie's mother is an inventor. She has invented a robot that carries the shopping from the car to the house and puts it away in the right places.

Imagine how the robot might work. Write an explanation. Use the clauses and conjunctions on page 19 to help you. Each sentence must have at least two clauses.

The robot uses its arms and grippers to lift the shopping out of the car, then

_____

_____

_____

_____

_____

_____

How did you do?

the robot has two long arms with grippers like hands

as if

or

although

and

it can pick things up just like a human

before

at the bottom is a big box

if

in its head there is a small computer

the robot can carry all the shopping

even though

when

as

after

but

as soon as

it puts it in the freezer

in order to

at the bottom is a big box

whereas

it starts sorting the shopping

until

it puts it in the fridge

there are rollers on its base

so

it scans the storage instructions

just as

because

whenever

then

while

unless

in case

it can roll into the house

it puts it in the cupboard

so that

How did you do?

Whose apostrophe?

For singular nouns add **'s** to the end of the word that own something. **Bob's shoe**.

Rewrite these noun phrases using nouns with apostrophes.

For example: the shed belonging to my mum = my mum's shed

1. the captain of the football team = _____

2. the armchair belonging to my dad = _____

3. the roof of the building = _____

4. the gold medal of Mo Farah = _____

5. the laptop bought by the teacher = _____

6. the mayor of the town = _____

7. the house owned by Mr Bliss = _____

8. the cover of the book = _____

9. the basket belonging to her cat = _____

10. the strange smile of Mrs James = _____

11. the tail of the mouse = _____

12. the name of the band = _____

How did you do?

Plurals with apostrophes

For plural nouns that end in **s** just add an apostrophe. **The buses' wheels**. If it doesn't end in **s** add **'s**.

Rewrite these noun phrases using nouns with apostrophes.

For example: the names of his friends = his friends' names

1. the leaders of the communities = _____

2. the house belonging to the two poets = _____

3. the playpen belonging to the babies = _____

4. the bikes belonging to the twins = _____

5. the treehouse belonging to the children = _____

6. the antlers of the deer = _____

7. the toilet for women = _____

8. the club for ladies = _____

9. the club for men = _____

10. the agreement of the gentlemen = _____

11. the tails of the mice = _____

12. the smell of the cheese = _____

How did you do?

Missing apostrophes

Put in the missing apostrophes.

1. Tim was using his mums computer.

2. The goats chewed Liams homework and his friends jacket.

3. On holiday we lost Dads trainers and the twins football boots.

4. We gazed at the peacocks beautiful tails.

5. The lilies white flowers had six long stamens
   with dark orange pollen at their tips.

6. Casss hobby is spinning sheeps wool to weave mats.

7. I saw a fishs fin that might have been a sharks.

8. Babies, childrens and adults shoes were all on special offer in the sale.

9. It is nobodys business what you do but somebodys eyes might be on you.

10. Out in the sea we could see the ferries lights and hear the gulls cries.

11. The Joness dogs teeth sank into the postmans ankle.

12. The Beatles songs were Grannys favourites when she was young but the
    Spice Girls songs were Mums choice.

How did you do?

Where have all the apostrophes gone?

Read the passage. Put in the missing apostrophes.

To Mr Parsonss surprise, a woman came into his shop with a parrot on her shoulder. There was a sign saying that dogs were not allowed but there was nothing about customers parrots.

When the parrots owner got to the checkout the shops computer wasn't working. The cashiers solution was to add up the ladys bill in his head.

"That will be £25.50, please," he said.

To everyones amazement, the parrot said, "The fish smells terrible. It should be half price!"

Now Mr Parsonss childrens greatest wish was to have a talking parrot, but this ones skills were something special. He wove his way through peoples baskets to hear the parrots voice more clearly.

"Let me have the parrot and your shopping is free," said Mr Parsons.

"£500," came the parrots voice, and the deal was done.

To the Parsons familys disappointment, the parrot never spoke again. A year later, the woman came back and asked about her old pets health.

"Take me home!" cried Polly from the shops stockroom, "This man is a monster!"

"This is very odd," said Mr Parsons.

"She needs to hear a friends voice," said the woman, whose name was Mary. "Perhaps she is missing her first home."

How did you do?

Spot the mistake (1)

Underline any words with incorrect apostrophes.

Write the words correctly underneath.

Maggie's Cafe
Mums' old recipe's and even
some of Grans' dishes'

_____

_____

My Ladys' Chamber
Fine bed linen from French maker's
No mixture's, just 100% cotton
straight from the makers looms

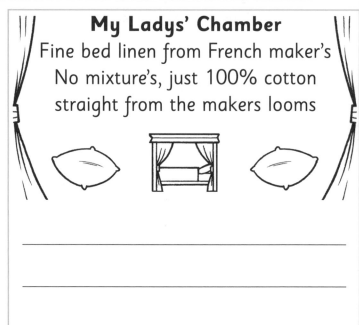

_____

_____

Pat's Perfumery
Fragrance's for all
His and her's
All the top brands, including
Georgio Bananis' latest

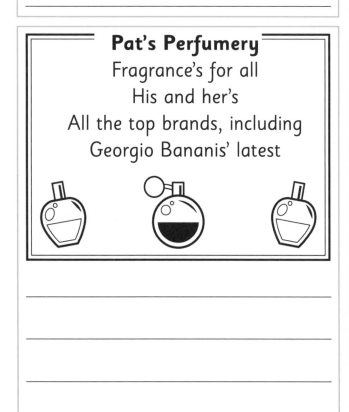

_____

_____

_____

_____

Ginger's Computer Genius's
Your virus's cleared
Our technicians's skills can sort your
computer's problem's
Expert tuition – at our office or your's

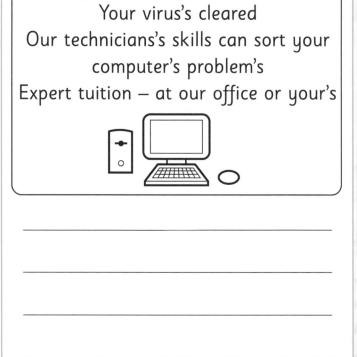

_____

_____

_____

_____

How did you do?

Absent apostrophes (1)

Read the passage.

Put in the missing apostrophes.

It was Joshs first day at his new school. This wasn't any old school but a magicians training centre. His parents idea of a good school was one that taught a lot of maths and English, but that wasn't his idea. When Josh tried to read, the books pages always seemed the wrong way around and for him the words meanings were never right.

His new teachers name was Aldo al Trix. In Aldo al Trixs class a lot of children couldn't read. The childrens maths books were full of instructions for tricks. Some of the tricks details included some very clever timing. Everyones school bag had a stopwatch in it and Year 4s stopwatch skills were soon second to none. The watchs numbers were a mystery to Josh at first. At the terms end came the headmistresss inspection.

"Please time the intervals between my eyes blinks, to the nearest thousandth of a second," were Ms Spellbinders words. Josh did it!

The classs main reading book was for new magicians – *Beginners Magic Tricks*. It was full of long words but by the end of the year Josh could read it.

He was really looking forward to the following years course, when the childrens main task would be to learn The Alfonsinis 'Sawing Ladies Heads Off' trick, in which no one was harmed. There would also be Marvells 'Magic Handkerchiefs'. In this trick the handkerchiefs disappearance was especially magic because it reappeared out of the audiences noses.

How did you do?

Apostrophe rewrite

Rewrite each sentence using apostrophes to show possession.

For example: This is the car of Max. ⟶ This is Max's car.

1. Who is the brother of Amy?

_____

2. Where are the footballs belonging to the teams?

_____

3. The beaks belonging to the geese are bright yellow.

_____

4. The answer is the guess of anyone.

_____

5. The nest of the mice is under the stairs.

_____

6. The leaves of the tree were long and thin.

_____

7. The natural habitat of a deer is woodland or scrub.

_____

8. The sound of the hooves of the horses was like thunder.

_____

How did you do?

Plural possessives

Change the nouns followed by brackets to the plural.

You might need to change or delete some other words.

> **For example:** The **girl's** (girls') writing was very untidy and **her** (their) **book's** (books') **cover** (covers) **was** (were) tattered.

1. The **man's** (_____) **face** (_____) **appeared**

   at the window.

2. The **fire engine's** (_____ _____) **siren** (_____)

   sounded through the **town's** (_____) **street** (_____).

3. The **mouse's** (_____) **tail** (_____) **was** (_____)

   very long.

4. The **bank's** (_____) doors were

   like a **castle's** (_____) gates.

5. The **boy's** (_____) diaries described

   the **bully's** (_____) attacks.

6. **A person's** (_____) health depends a lot on **his or her**

   (_____) diet.

7. **A child's** (_____) **teacher** (_____) can make a big

   difference to the **child's** (_____) learning.

How did you do?

Missing owners

Write nouns in the gaps, with apostrophes to show possession.

At least one noun in each sentence must be plural.

For example: I don't like the **Jones's** dog but the **Smiths'** dog is much nicer.

1.   In the valley there were cows in most of the _____ fields.

2.   After cleaning her _____ boots, Cinderella needed to repair her _____ dresses.

3.   We could see the _____ cat in the _____ tree.

4.   We were going to stay at the _____ hotel but it was too expensive so we stayed at the _____ inn.

5.   The _____ office is on the ground floor but the _____ cloakroom is on the first floor.

6.   There were mice and gerbils in the pet shop, so I went to find out about the _____ food and the _____ cages.

7.   _____ presents were under the Christmas tree but the _____ presents were in stockings at the bottom of their beds.

8.   Lots of animals lived in the old oak tree: there were several _____ nests in its branches, a _____ home in a hole in the trunk and a _____ den at the bottom.

How did you do?

Absent apostrophes (2)

At last it was the day for our classs outing to Patti Parrs Wonderful World of Plants and Animals. The attractions amazing exhibits were housed in huge greenhouses. In the first greenhouse was a display of magical fungi. One funguss stalk was ten metres high and its canopy was two metres wide; anothers pattern had multi-coloured triangles and circles; but the fungis special magic was to turn their pattern into someones face. One fungus changed its pattern into my mate Bobby Butlers face!

One greenhouses magical display was a set of talking cacti. The cactis voices copied ours – and there were plenty for them to copy. One cactuss voice sounded just like our teachers when she is telling us off.

The amazing animal centres main attraction was a talking ox. We watched the oxs mouth (and the farmers) to make sure it was really the oxs voice. The other oxens skills were different: they could balance coins on their hooves tips or dance to the tune of the farmers fiddle.

As well as mammals, the animal centres collection included fish, such as the ten jumping salmon. The salmons bodies could flick and twist in amazing formations. Even the almost invisible tiny creatures called plankton could do tricks. To see the planktons tricks we watched through microscope viewers.

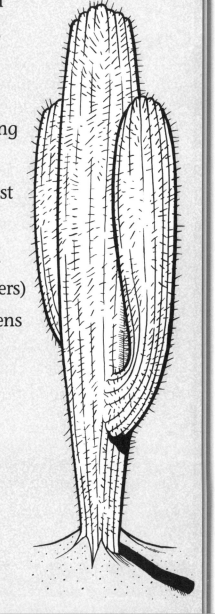

How did you do?

Spot the mistake (2)

Read the menu for Claude's Cafe.

Underline any words with incorrect or missing apostrophes.

Write the word correctly in the box.

Claude's Café
CAFE

Claude's cafe menu

Starter's
The chefs special mushrooms' with garlic
Prawns in scallops shells with creamy sauce
His and her's spare rib's — share with friends'

Main courses
Claudes fillet steak on a bed of mushroom's
with green bean's
Fish pie made with three different fish's

Desserts
Madame Claudes' French pastry's
Ice cream in many flavour's

Drinks'
All kinds of coffee or tea
Soft drink's

How did you do?

Pronouns

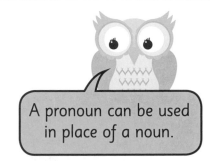

A pronoun can be used in place of a noun.

Underline the pronouns.

1. My mum lost her purse on the way to meet her friend for lunch.

2. We wondered where our fish had gone because they were not in the tank.

3. Our cat looked very happy and was licking its lips.

4. The astronaut knew which helmet was hers because it had her name on it.

5. Our brother spends most of his time playing with his train set.

6. It was our fault, not theirs.

7. Shall we meet at your house or mine?

8. "It's bed time," said our mum, but we asked her if we could finish our game first.

9. That's the last time I'll ride my bike without wearing my helmet, because I could have injured my head when I fell off.

10. This is where I found your phone, still in its box. I knew it was yours right away.

11. It's our sister's birthday today and this is her present from us.

12. The traffic warden got out his pad, wrote out a ticket and put it on the car.

13. "That's mine!" said Simon, snatching his toy car from his friend.

How did you do?

The possessors

Write a possessive pronoun to complete the second sentence.

Check that each one makes sense.

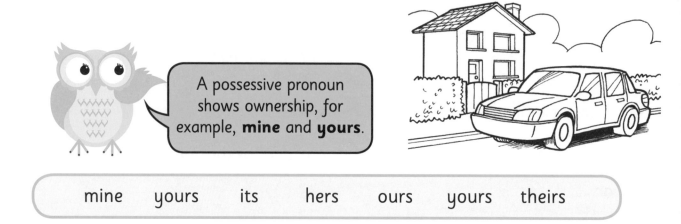

A possessive pronoun shows ownership, for example, **mine** and **yours**.

| | mine | yours | its | hers | ours | yours | theirs | |

1.	The car belongs to Mr Green.	The car is _____.
2.	The shoes belong to the woman.	The shoes are _____.
3.	The basket belongs to the cat.	The basket is _____.
4.	The tablet belongs to Ella.	The tablet is _____.
5.	The book belongs to us.	The book is _____.
6.	The toy belongs to you	The toy is _____.
7.	The dresses belong to me.	The dresses are _____.

How did you do?

Get possessive

Write the correct pronouns in the gaps.

For example: He put on his coat but when he looked closely I wasn't sure if it really was <u>his</u>.

1. Class 4B always enjoyed their maths lessons but Class 4a didn't

enjoy _____.

2. I took out my book but when I looked closely I wasn't sure if it really

was _____.

3. Sandeep put on his coat and helped his little brother to put

on _____.

4. I ate my breakfast but my sister didn't eat _____.

5. We wore our wellies but the others didn't wear _____.

6. This drink is _____ and that one is _____.

7. I'm the one who plays the piano so it is

my piano. The piano is _____.

8. Nina got the drums for her birthday so they

are her drums They are _____.

How did you do?

Repeated nouns

Circle any nouns you think should be replaced by pronouns.

Rewrite the passage using the correct pronouns.

May sat on May's chair. Tara wanted to sit there but May said that she should sit on Tara's chair. Tom got on with Tom's work and wondered why May didn't let Tara have May's chair. She could have sat on Tara's chair, after all.

Mr Ravel came to see what May, Tara and Tom were talking about. He asked if they were discussing May, Tara and Tom's maths problem. May and Tara said, "Yes." Tom looked at them and said, "No. We were talking about chairs."

How did you do?

Spot the verbs

Underline the verbs in the passage below.

Dear Diary

Our class read a poem called 'The Listeners' by Walter de la Mare. It told the story of a man who rode a horse through some woods at night. He stopped at a castle. I guessed that because the poem said, 'a bird flew out of the turret'. The man knocked on the door three times but no one answered. Perhaps ghosts were listening. The poet called them 'phantom listeners'.

He waited and his horse chomped the grass. Every sound echoed. Then the traveller called out. He said he had kept his word. He had promised to come.

Nobody answered so he rode off into the woods.

I wonder where the traveller went. Where did he sleep? I made up a story about him. In my story he knocked at the door of another house. A man opened the door and said, "You have been to the castle. They were there last night. Someone came on a horse. He went into the castle. He didn't come out. Nobody came out."

The traveller went back to the castle. He knocked. Then he tried the door. It opened so he tied his horse to a tree and went in. He entered a big hall with a staircase that twisted up the wall. Then he spotted a doorway that led into a big room. A huge table nearly filled the room. A banquet was set out on it. Nobody had eaten the food.

Then the traveller gasped. Around the table in the big carved chairs sat six ghosts. The ghosts were watching him. They all wore riding capes. The ghost of a horse stood behind each. They looked just the same as his horse.

The man backed out of the room and ran outside. His horse had gone.

How did you do?

Vivid verbs

Rewrite the sentences using more interesting verbs.
See what 'pictures' you can make readers imagine.

You might find it helpful to underline the verbs first.

1. An old man was under the bridge.

_____

2. A car came down the road.

_____

3. Four scruffy boys were sitting on the park bench.

_____

4. The old man got up from his chair.

_____

5. She put the box on the step and looked at me.

_____

6. "He's the man who broke the window," she said.

_____

7. She took a cake from the plate and put it in her mouth.

_____

8. I picked up the paper and put it in the bin.

_____

How did you do?

Tense station

The tenses are either past or present.

Write in the boxes, the verb and tense on the signs.

14.00	Birmingham

There is no buffet on
this train.

14.05	Leeds

The 14.05 from Leeds
has been delayed.

15.03	Durham

The next train to Durham
will leave platform 2 at 15.03.

13.00	Delayed

The 13.00 from London
is running 45 minutes late.

Information

Passengers are asked not to
leave luggage unattended.

13.45	York

The train arriving at platform
6 is the 13.45 to york.

13.55	Arrived

The train that has just arrived at platform 1 is the 13.55
from Durham. This train terminates here.

How did you do?

Writing past tense verbs

Write each verb in the present and past tenses as shown in the examples.

Verb	Present tense	Past tense
fall	he is falling	he was falling
slip	we are slipping	
fight	they are fighting	
hop	I	
hope	he	
chase	they	
trick	you	
try	we	
lead	I	
follow	you	
create	it	
do	we	
manage	they	
notice	he	
arrange	you	
flee	I	
agree	he	
cycle	she	
whine	it	
write	he	
bake	they	

How did you do?

erbs and nouns

Another past

Write the present and past tenses of each verb as shown in the examples.

Verb	Present tense	Past tense
walk	I walk	I walked
stop	he stops	
use	we use	
sing	you	
bring	she	
fling	I	
run	they	
eat	he	
hide	it	
ride	we	
slide	they	
glide	I	
come	you	
cling	he	
keep	she	
sleep	it	
drive	they	
arrive	we	
sink	it	
drink	I	
think	she	

How did you do?

Into the past

Rewrite the verbs in brackets in the correct past tense.

1. There (are) _____ ten green bottles standing on a wall.

2. No one (knows) _____ who (leaves) _____ them there.

3. One green bottle accidentally (falls) _____ and

   (breaks) _____.

4. That (means) _____ there (are) _____ nine left.

5. Another bottle (drops) _____ off, so eight (remain) _____.

6. No one (sees) _____ what (makes) _____ them fall.

7. This (continue) _____ until no bottle

   (stands) _____ on the wall.

8. A lot of broken glass (litters) _____ the

   ground until someone (recycles) _____ it.

9. Then someone (writes) _____ a song about the bottles.

10. Teachers everywhere (teach) _____ it to children.

11. The children (learn) _____ number bonds to ten.

12. My class (rejoice) _____ that the mystery person

    (provides) _____ only ten bottles because we (progress)

    _____ to numbers past 1000, without singing about bottles.

How did you do?

Back to the past

Rewrite these sentences in the past tense.
Check that all the verbs are correct.

1. I don't know where my brother is hiding.

_____

2. I'm knocking on the door and I can hear someone coming.

_____

3. Someone asks who is there and I wonder if this is a joke, so I say, "Teresa."

_____

4. A voice inside asks if I'm being funny, so I say, "Yes."

_____

5. "All right – Teresa who?" asks the voice and I hear a loud tut.

_____

6. It's my brother and he doesn't recognise my voice because I'm disguising it.

_____

7. "Teresa in the woods," I reply and my brother guesses who it is.

_____

8. He guesses because, he says, no one else tells such silly jokes.

_____

How did you do?

Putting the past right

Correct any incorrect verbs. Write the correct words above them.

After checking that I'd washt my neck, Mum tolled me that my manners

wasn't good enough. Maybe if I improvd them I could ask for more pocket

money. So at breakfast I stud up and gave my mum my chair, past her a

cup of tea and spended the whole meal saying please and thank you. The

meal seemd to take ages. I was just about manageing to eat in between

politeness. Then Dad seen me speaking with my mouth full when I tryed

to eat and say thank you at the same time. However, he guest what I was

trieing to do and laught. I lookt at Mum out of the corner of my eye but she

pretendid not to notice.

I wisht there was an easier way to be polite. Then I spoted Dad's empty

plate. He had eaten and say please and thank you a lot. How? I watcht.

What he done was to take smaller mouthfuls. Well, he haven't died of

malnutrition from being polite, so it's worth a try.

How did you do?

Write the verb

Write the verbs in brackets in the past tense.

Check that you have chosen the correct form of past tense.

For example: We **went** to town or We **were going** to town

---

SUNTOWN GAZETTE
MYSTERY ILLNESS STRIKES!

Sunshine Primary School (to cancel) _____ some classes this morning because a mysterious illness (to strike) _____ many of its teachers. The school (to provide) _____ lessons for Years 1, 2 and 3 but (to ask) _____ parents of children in Years 4, 5 and 6 not to send them to school. The school (to arrange) _____ for other teachers to take over as soon as possible. Some children (to say) _____ that they (to enjoy) _____ having a day off but (to miss) _____ playing football. The school (to face) _____ another problem last week when thieves (to steal) _____ the lead from the roof. Heavy rain (to fall) _____ during the night. This (to cause) _____ flooding in some classrooms and (to damage) _____ a computer. Staff and children (to tidy) _____ up, and (to carry on) _____ as normal. The Suntown Gazette (to donate) _____ a new computer to the Year 4 class.

How did you do?

Writing the past

Read the story of the poem 'The Listeners' (on page 35)

What do you think had happened to the six people and horses who were ghosts in the castle? What do you think happened next?

Continue the story using interesting verbs in the different forms of past tense. Underline the verbs.

appear	arrive	change	creep	depart	transform
watch	die	enter	escape	fade	slink
fight	whinny	hide	kill	leave	listen
	neigh	trap	seize	snatch	

The man turned this way and that. Then _____

_____

_____

_____

_____

_____

_____

_____

_____

_____

How did you do?

Determine the nouns

A determiner is a word like **a**, **the**, **some**. It goes before a noun.

Put a determiner before each noun. (Not all these words can be nouns.)

_____ cherry	_____ help	_____ make
_____ when	_____ eat	_____ play
_____ by	_____ white	_____ strike
_____ choice	_____ large	_____ slowly
_____ this	_____ clap	_____ run
_____ hurry	_____ bring	_____ empty
_____ under	_____ see	_____ ask
_____ quality	_____ miserable	_____ ending
_____ bake	_____ wicked	_____ trick
_____ leave	_____ untidy	_____ patient

Write six sentences using some of the nouns.

_____

_____

_____

_____

_____

_____

How did you do?

Determiners making a difference

Write a determiner in each gap.

a   an   the   some

What is _____ time?

It's time you got _____ watch!

What's worse than finding _____ maggot in _____ apple you've just bitten?

Finding half of one!

Waiter! There's _____ fly in my soup.

It's OK, _____ spider on _____ roll will catch it.

Would you like _____ ox-tongue sandwich?

I'm not eating anything that's come from _____ animal's mouth. I'll have eggs.

How did you do?

46

Singular and plural determiners

Rewrite each sentence, making the underlined words plural.

1. <u>This is</u> the <u>house</u> that Jack built.

_____

2. The school bought <u>a camera</u> and <u>an tablet</u>.

_____

3. <u>That child is</u> very bad-mannered.

_____

4. What <u>is that elephant</u> doing in the <u>fridge</u>?

_____

5. I know who <u>this man is</u> but not <u>that woman</u>.

_____

6. I bought <u>a book</u> and <u>a felt-tipped pen</u> yesterday and <u>a pencil</u> today.

_____

7. <u>This girl</u> won <u>a race</u> and took home <u>a</u> very nice <u>prize</u>.

_____

8. I like <u>this jumper</u>, <u>this shirt</u> and <u>that jacket</u>.

_____

How did you do?

Determination

Write determiners that make sense in the gaps. Use the words to help you.

| a | all | an | any | both | each | this |
| every | no | some | that | the | those | these |

Jason could see Tom outside eating _____ orange. He wondered if it

was _____ orange that had disappeared from his lunch box. He had

two pieces of fruit – _____ pear and _____ orange. Now he had

none because _____ fruits had gone.

"I bet _____ orange is _____ one that was

in my lunch box," he thought.

Mark gave Jason _____ apple and said,

"Here have _____ apple. I have two and

you don't have _____ fruit."

Reeta said, "Last term I had _____ fruit at all for lunch because

someone took _____ piece from my lunch box. That wasn't _____

healthy diet but I have _____ grapes today. Here, have one of

_____ grapes."

The next day, Jason's mum gave him _____ extra fruit and said,

"Offer _____ piece to Tom. You have fruit _____ day. Perhaps he

never has fruit in his lunch box."

How did you do?

Describe the noun

Make a noun phrase by adding a determiner and a word to describe each noun.

For example: cat – a fat cat

Use 'a' or 'an' infront of your descriptive word for each picture.

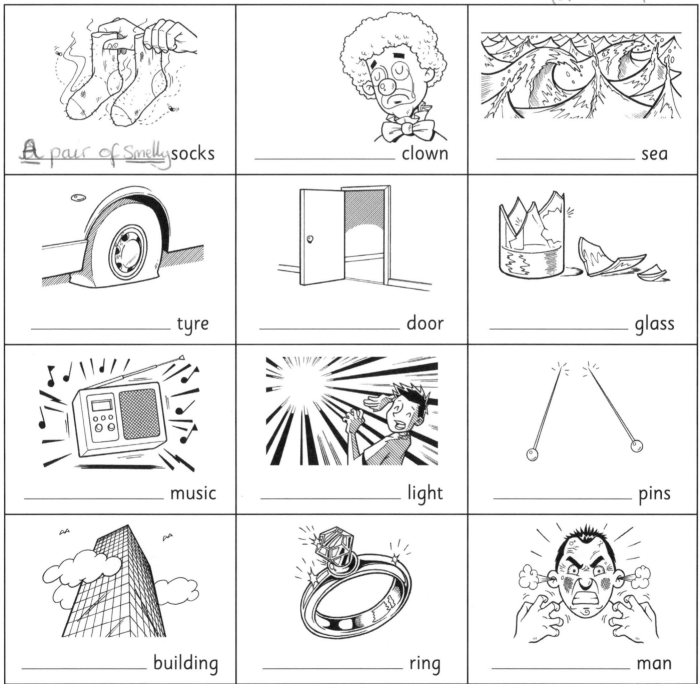

A pair of smelly socks

_____ clown

_____ sea

_____ tyre

_____ door

_____ glass

_____ music

_____ light

_____ pins

_____ building

_____ ring

_____ man

How did you do?

Build a noun phrase

Underline the noun in the first sentence in each set.

Then add a word, then another and so on.

1a. I found a shell.

1b. I found a _____ shell.

1c. I found a _____ _____ shell.

1d. I found a _____ _____ _____ shell.

> Add word, about its size.

> Add another word, about its colour.

> Add another word, about its shape.

2a. A car stopped outside.

2b. A _____ car stopped outside.

2c. A _____ _____ car stopped outside.

2d. A _____ _____ car _____ stopped outside.

> Add word, about its colour.

> Add another word, about its size.

> Add some more words about the car.

3a. I like _____ cream.

3b. I like _____ cream.

3c. I like _____ cream _____.

3d. I like _____ cream _____.

> Add a word to say what kind of cream.

> Add another word, about its flavour.

> Add some more words to say what you like with it.

> Add some more words to say what else you like with it.

How did you do?

Noun phrase hunt

Draw a loop around each noun phrase.

Then underline the main noun in the noun phrase.

For example: (A bright blue <u>butterfly</u>) landed on (the purple <u>flower</u>.)

1. A large ginger cat crept along the garden wall.

2. I flopped down onto the big, comfortable sofa.

3. Wasps' nests look like hollow balls of thin white paper.

4. We have three small brown hens.

5. We watched as enormous waves crashed onto the little boats.

6. A large heavy brown package flopped through the letterbox.

7. You can't turn a sow's ear into a silk purse.

8. They followed the long winding path through the dense woods.

9. I am returning this absolutely useless hairdryer.

10. We watched a television programme about some young divers who found a complete Viking ship.

11. The bright, colourful fireworks lit up the dark night sky.

12. In the old poem, the wise owl and the beautiful cat sailed away in a beautiful pea-green boat.

How did you do?

Expanded noun phrases

Add one or more words to each noun to make expanded noun phrases. You might need to change the determiners.

1. One _____ day in January we made a _____ snowman.

2. Osman's _____ sister played _____ music on

   the _____ piano.

3. Two _____ men were coming down the _____ street towards us.

4. Sarah got her _____ bike out of the _____ shed.

5. As we entered the _____ hall I noticed a

   _____ clock high up on the _____ wall.

6. The _____ cupboard is full of _____

   shoes, _____ socks and _____ toys.

7. In the _____ fable, the _____ tortoise

   won the race against the _____ hare.

8. In another _____ fable a _____ lion

   made friends with a _____ mouse.

How did you do?

Changing the mood

Rewrite this description, to give a different impression of the place.

Change the bold words in the noun phrases.

You could add extra words to these noun phrases.

A row of **brightly painted snug little** houses faced the **calm blue** sea. Each one had a **small rectangular** garden with a **tidy** lawn and **neat** flowerbeds. **Some hard-working** harbour workers were taking a **short** break for a **small** lunch. The fishermen were out in their **sturdy old** boats. **Not many** villagers had time to sit in the **ancient** Lobster Pot inn for **a few** drinks and **tasty, fresh** sandwiches. Visitors, wearing **new summer** clothes and talking loudly, took up the **comfortable** seats in its **pleasant** garden. The **friendly** landlord always gave a **cheerful** greeting and **excellent** service.

How did you do?

Writing with noun phrases

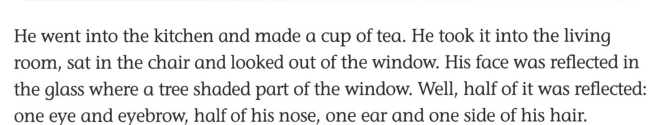

Remember that you can add words before or after the noun – or both.

Rewrite the passage, making some of the nouns into noun phrases to say what the man and the scene were like.

He went into the kitchen and made a cup of tea. He took it into the living room, sat in the chair and looked out of the window. His face was reflected in the glass where a tree shaded part of the window. Well, half of it was reflected: one eye and eyebrow, half of his nose, one ear and one side of his hair.

After washing his cup in the sink he took down his jacket from the hook in the hall, put it on, picked up the door key from its hook and went out. He locked the door, went down the garden path and turned right along the road.

How did you do?

Write your own description

Use the passage on page 54 to help you to write a few paragraphs about someone you have watched.

Begin by writing nouns you will use on the mind map below.

Then build these into noun phrases that say what the person is like.

Add more ovals and lines if you need them.

Write nouns in the ovals and words to make noun phrases along the lines.

How did you do?

How, when and where?

Underline the adverbial in each sentence.

Decide what each adverbial says about the verb.

Write **how**, **when** or **where** on the line.

> An adverbial acts like an adverb. It gives more information about a verb.

For example: The children got up <u>before dawn</u>.   _____when_____

Adverbial tells us:

1. She ran like the wind.   _____

2. There's an elephant in the classroom.   _____

3. The spider climbed up the spout.   _____

4. It is going to rain all week.   _____

5. Hedgehogs must hug one another with great care.   _____

6. A flock of birds flew over the village   _____

7. She swims like a fish   _____

8. I'll phone at seven o'clock.   _____

9. We didn't hear a sound during the night.   _____

10. Never keep elephants in the fridge   _____

11. The teacher spoke in a friendly voice.   _____

12. She caught the ball with both hands.   _____

13. I looked at the mess with a sinking feeling.   _____

How did you do?

More about the verbs

Circle the verbs in these sentences.

Underline the adverbials that say more about the verbs.

1. Two eggs in a pan looked at one another with frightened expressions.

2. Water was turning into steam all around them.

3. Then a girl came along with a spoon.

4. One of the eggs tried as hard as it could to get onto the spoon.

5. The other said in a sharp voice, "That's not a lifebelt."

6. The other asked in a frightened voice what it was for.

7. The answer came in a flash: "For bashing us over the head!"

8. The eggs in the carton were watching all the while.

9. They muttered for a long time and decided what to do, as if with one mind.

10. In their own secret way they got a message to the hens.

11. The hens clucked in horror.

12. After that they laid their eggs in a secret place.

How did you do?

Poetic adverbials

Read the poem. Look for the verbs. Then look for any adverbials.
On the chart write the adverbials and what say about the verbs.

Bed in Summer
by Robert Louis Stevenson

In winter I get up at night
And dress by yellow candle light.
In summer, quite the other way,
I have to go to bed by day.

I have to go to bed and see
The birds still hopping on the tree,
Or hear the grown-up people's feet
Still going past me in the street.

And does it not seem hard to you,
When all the sky is clear and blue,
And I should like so much to play,
To have to go to bed by day?

Verb	Adverbials	What they tell us about the verb
get up	at night	when the child gets up
dress		
go (in verse 1)	1) 2)	1) 2)
go (in verse 2)		
hopping		
going past		

How did you do?

Catch an adverbial

Use an adverbial from a fish to complete each sentence.

1. I can see two fish swimming _____.

2. I have been fishing _____.

3. Sometimes I wade _____.

4. Anglers _____ have to wait _____.

5. When I'm fishing I sit _____.

6. It's best to start _____.

7. I met my friend here _____.

8. I caught two big salmon _____.

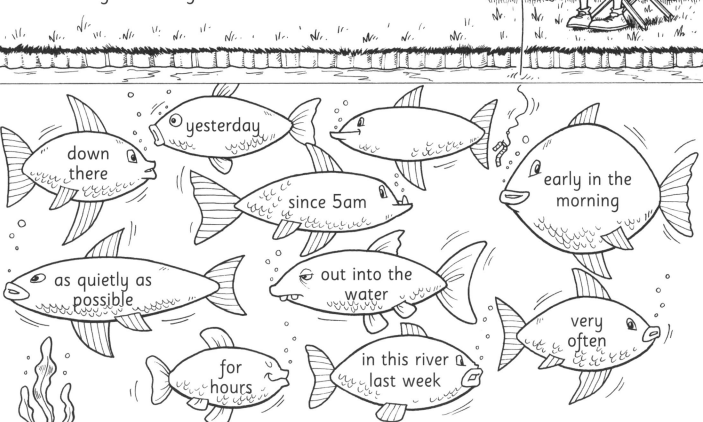

down there

yesterday

since 5am

early in the morning

as quietly as possible

out into the water

very often

for hours

in this river last week

How did you do?

Moving to the front

Underline the adverbial in each sentence.

Rewrite the sentence with the adverbial at the beginning.

1. She crept along the corridor as quietly as possible.

_____

2. There were hundreds of stalls at the fair.

_____

3. We go to the farmers' market on Saturdays.

_____

4. There's a traffic jam on the motorway every morning.

_____

5. He cut out the shapes as carefully as possible.

_____

6. I watched the fireworks from my bedroom window.

_____

7. The boy ran down the lane as if his life depended on it.

_____

8. He poured out the drinks without a single spill.

_____

How did you do?

Adverbials for you

Each sentence begins with an adverbial.

Complete each sentence, choosing a verb from the box to help you.

finished	kicked	posed	stood
ate	visited	found	disappeared
jumped	will confiscate	fell	sat

1. After four hours, _____.

2. With a hoot of laughter, _____.

3. In the twinkling of an eye, _____.

4. At the top of the hill _____.

5. On holiday, _____.

6. Before the football match, _____.

7. With perfect balance, _____.

8. Under the stone, _____.

9. In no time at all, _____.

10. At the table _____.

11. At that moment, _____.

12. In future, _____.

How did you do?

Your own adverbials

Write an adverbial in each gap to say more about the verb.

'Where?', 'When?' and 'How?'

1. _____ I could see a squirrel.

2. _____ the man greeted his friend.

3. _____ the sun came out.

4. _____ no one will be allowed into this room.

5. _____ he had finished his work.

6. _____ my dad buys a newspaper.

7. _____ the boat was missing _____.

8. _____ the bluebells grew _____.

9. _____ he jumped _____.

10. _____ my brother swims _____.

11. _____ George walked _____.

12. _____ we saw farmers working _____.

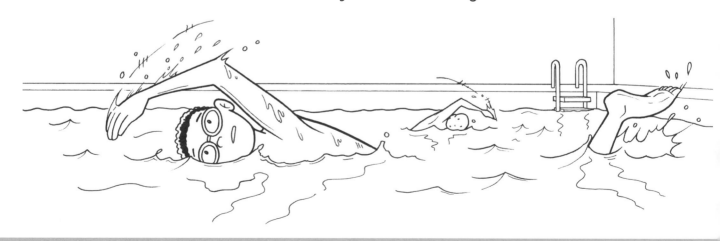

How did you do?

Writing with adverbials

Write a newspaper report about Jack and Jill.

THE HILLSIDE TIMES Friday 12 May

CHILDREN IN SERIOUS ACCIDENT

On Sunday two young children _____

_____

_____

_____

_____

_____

_____

_____

_____

_____

How did you do?

Pronoun search (1)

Underline each pronoun and write the noun it replaces above it.

It was Tim's first day in his new job as hotel receptionist. The manager was giving him some training. He told him to greet all guests by their names. He said that this would make them feel welcome.

"How will I know their names?" he asked.

"You can find them for yourself. Read the labels on their bags," replied the manager.

Just then some guests arrived, so he left the receptionist to greet them.

The manager listened from his office and heard him greeting the guests:

"Good morning Mr Real Leather. Good morning, Ms Polyester. I hope you enjoy yourselves here."

The manager shook his head and decided that he would greet the next guests himself.

How did you do?

Pronoun search (2)

Underline each pronoun and write the noun it replaces above it.

A family of five arrived at the hotel late at night. It had 500 floors and their room was on the top floor.

The lift was broken, so to amuse themselves as they climbed the stairs, Dad said, "We'll take turns to tell stories and jokes for 100 floors each. I'll go first."

They started up the steps, with Dad telling his favourite 'knock, knock' joke, then his second favourite, then all the others he knew. They had all heard them before.

The children each took a turn at telling their favourite funny stories. Then, after two hours, they reached the 400th floor and it was Mum's turn. She put her hand in her pocket and went rather quiet. Then she said, "I have a sad story. I left the keys for our room in reception."

How did you do?

Pronouns for nouns

Underline all the nouns. Decide which ones can be replaced by a pronoun.

Write the pronoun in the space above the noun.

Only change pronouns if it's clear who or what they mean.

Samantha was on holiday in Spain. Samantha went into a restaurant and ordered Samantha's lunch. Samantha asked for a mushroom omelette. The waiter brought Samantha's omelette but there were no mushrooms in the omelette. Samantha didn't speak Spanish and the waiter didn't speak much English. So Samantha drew a picture of a mushroom and showed it to the waiter. Samantha made signs to ask the waiter to bring some mushrooms. The waiter went off, scratching the waiter's head.

The waiter came back and gave Samantha an umbrella.

"Why have you brought the umbrella?" Samantha asked.

The waiter pointed to Samantha's drawing and said, "You ask. I bring."

Samantha pointed to the omelette, so the waiter put the umbrella on the omelette.

Samantha got very cross and said that Samantha might as well cook the omelette Samantha's self.

Another customer told Samantha that Samantha should take lessons in drawing and Spanish.

How did you do?

Make it clear with pronouns

Rewrite the passage.

Replace some pronouns with nouns if it is not clear what they mean.

One day Moss the Border Collie was in the hall when it came through the letter box. He grabbed it and ran out through the back door and dropped it at his feet. He laughed and put it back through the letter box. He did the same again. So he put it in a plant pot by the door and went on to deliver the mail to the next house.

He ran after him with it in his mouth and dropped it at his feet, wagging his tail.

He gave up, put it back in his trolley and went on to the next house. Then he saw him take a letter out of it and run off, wagging his tail. He ran after him. He took it to a house along the road and put it on the step. She opened the door and picked it up.

"Thank you," she said.

"How did he know it was for her?" he asked himself.

_____

_____

_____

_____

_____

_____

_____

How did you do?

Ambiguous pronouns

Underline the pronouns that may cause confusion and need to be changed to nouns. Rewrite each text so that the meaning is clear.

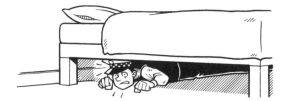

1. A police officer found the burglar.

He was hiding under the bed.

2. Our beauty tip of the day reveals how to keep your skin soft. Cut it out and keep it on your dressing table.

3. Children are damaging these gardens. We blame their parents. They play chasing games here.

4. I'd recognise that woman anywhere. She has a dog. She has big feet, long ears and sniffs lamp posts.

5. Dale said that she and Anna saw the ducks during their walk, adding that they were wearing waterproof boots.

6. If your child won't eat raw fruit chop it into small pieces.

How did you do?

Pronoun or noun?

Circle the correct noun, noun phrase or pronoun from the brackets.

Check that you don't repeat the nouns too often.

Check that the meaning of each pronoun is clear.

The Miser and his Gold – a fable by Aesop

Once upon a time there was a miser who buried (the man's, his, their, her) gold in a box in (the miser's, his, her, their) garden. Every week (the miser, she, he, they) would dig (him, her, the gold, it) up and gloat over (she, he, they, it).

One day a robber was watching. A few days later (he, the miser, the robber, they) dug (it, him, them) up and ran off with (him, them, it, the gold). The next time (he, the miser) came to gloat over (the miser's, the burglar's, his) treasures, (the miser, he, him) found nothing in (it, the box). (The miser, Him, He) cried out and (they, them, he, his neighbours) came to see what was wrong. (He, They, The miser) told them how (they, he, the miser) used to come and look at (his, her, their, the miser's) gold and that someone must have been watching.

"Did you ever spend any of (him, they, them, it)?" asked one of (them, they, the neighbours).

"No," (the miser, he, him) said. "(The miser, Me, I) just looked at (him, it, he, the gold)."

"Then come and look at (the hole, it, him)," (a neighbour, he) said. "(It, He, Him, They) will do (you, the miser, it, him) just as much good."

How did you do?

Pronouns to link sentences

Use pronouns to link the two sentences. Write the new sentence.

Example:

This is the house. Jack built this house.

This is the house that Jack built.

Linking pronouns

that   where

which   who

1. There was an old woman. The old woman swallowed a fly.

_____

2. There was an old woman. The old woman lived in a shoe.

_____

3. My grandmother has a garden. She grows roses in her garden.

_____

4. This is my new computer. It is much faster than my old one.

_____

5. There is the old car. It appeared in our garden last night.

_____

6. They went to live in Australia. They bought a hotel there.

_____

7. This is the malt. This malt lay in this house. Jack built this house.

_____

How did you do?

Pronoun progress

Edit the newspaper article. Use pronouns to make shorter sentences, join sentences and get rid of unnecessary words.

Write your edited article below.

RUNAWAY LAWNMOWER CAUSES HAVOC

On Friday afternoon Simon Tallgrass was cutting the grass in Simon Tallgrass's garden. Simon was using his new lawnmower. The lawnmower was a very powerful lawnmower. The lawnmower was the kind that you sit on.

Simon Tallgrass had not read all the instructions for Simon's new lawnmower. Simon Tallgrass had forgotten to read how to stop the lawnmower. Simon Tallgrass zoomed along the lawn on Simon's lawnmower. Simon came to Simon's very neat flowerbed. Simon's prize-winning carnations were growing in Simon's flowerbed. The lawnmower went straight through Simon's prize-winning carnations and into Simon's pond. Simon looked very silly sitting in Simon's pond.

_____

_____

_____

_____

_____

_____

_____

How did you do?

Making links

The words that make links between sentences in this passage are underlined. Complete the chart to show which words they link with.

Passage	What the words link with
We went to Spain for our holiday. We had a great time <u>there</u>.	Spain
We took sunhats and sun cream. <u>They</u> protected us from sunburn	sunhats and sun cream
The weather was sunny every day. <u>That</u> meant we could spend a lot of time on the beach.	the sunny weather
Mum said <u>it</u> made her feel very relaxed.	
On our last day <u>she</u> wanted to go to the shops.	
We caught the bus into the nearest town. <u>It</u> was full of little white houses	
We thought <u>they</u> were painted white to reflect the sunlight.	
<u>Afterwards</u> we packed our bags ready for going home.	
We left <u>them</u> in the lobby to be collected.	

How did you do?

Linkers

Circle the word that links the two sentences.

Draw a line to show which words it links to.

> **For example:**
>
> I went to the newsagent's to buy a comic. I was surprised to find that (they) didn't have (any.)

1. It's my brother's birthday tomorrow. I've bought a pen for him.

2. All through August the weather was wet. We hardly played outside because of it.

3. It was sunny in September. It was pity we had to go back to school then.

4. I tidied my bedroom on Saturday. Afterwards I could find a lot of the things I had lost.

5. There's a rainbow over the woods. Can you see the end of it?

6. We climbed the steps to the top of the tower. From there we could see the whole town.

7. I went to the leisure centre to meet my friend. I was sad that she wasn't there.

8. I've been saving my pocket money for a long time. I think I have enough to buy a Newcastle United shirt.

How did you do?

Paragraph summary

Read the text below. Then write a summary of each paragraph on the next sheet.

The Visitor

This is the story of 'The Visitor', a poem by Ian Serraillier. It begins with a man walking alone at night in a churchyard near the sea.

Earlier in the day, a violent storm had brought the sea crashing into the churchyard, overturning gravestones and tearing coffins and skeletons out of graves. The man spotted a skeleton with a beautiful ring on its bony finger.

He pulled the ring off the skeleton's finger and ran home with it. That night he gave it to his wife. She said it was the loveliest ring in the world, and asked him where he got it. He didn't say a word.

The couple went to bed and fell asleep. At midnight something woke them. They heard a voice in the darkness. It was asking for the ring. It seemed to be coming nearer. The frightened woman asked her husband what it was.

He said that there was nothing to worry about, but the voice came nearer. Then it said it was getting into the bed.

The woman screamed and pulled the sheet over her head. Something tore off the sheet and flung it aside. The voice shouted that it would drag the woman out of the bed.

Her husband told her to throw the ring away. She threw it as hard as she could. Soon after, there was a clatter. Something picked up the ring, jumped out of the window and clattered down the lane. The clattering faded, quieter and quieter. Then there was silence.

How did you do?

Write a summary of each paragraph of 'The Visitor' in note form. The first one has been done for you.

Paragraph 1	Sets scene for story of man in churchyard at night.
Paragraph 2	
Paragraph 3	
Paragraph 4	
Paragraph 5	
Paragraph 6	
Paragraph 7	

How did you do?

Link words in a story

Look closely at the story on page 74. Find the words listed on the chart that help us determine the links between the sentences.

They link the paragraph to the one before.

Make a note about what these words mean.

For example: (paragraph 2):

a violent storm had brought the sea crashing into <u>the</u> churchyard, overturning gravestones and tearing coffins and skeletons out of graves. <u>The</u> man spotted a skeleton with a beautiful ring on <u>its</u> bony finger.

Paragraph	Link word	What it links to
2	the the its	churchyard in paragraph 1 man in paragraph 1 the skeleton's
3	it	
4	it	
5	he it	
6	her it it	
7	it	

How did you do?

Organising paragraphs

Group the sentences below into three paragraphs for an information text.

Write them in the chart on the next page.

Hedgehogs in the garden

Hedgehogs usually hibernate between November and March.

Hedgehogs eat snails, slugs and insects.

Cover drains so that hedgehogs can't fall in and get trapped.

They sometimes sleep or hibernate in piles of wood or compost heaps, so check before burning rubbish or digging.

You can buy special hedgehog food or give them minced meat, tinned dog or cat food (but not fish) or chopped boiled eggs.

Put out a shallow bowl or saucer of fresh water in very dry weather.

Slug pellets can poison hedgehogs.

Put a few rocks near the edges of a pond to help hedgehogs climb out, so that they don't drown.

Hedgehogs often sleep under hedges or in long grass – so check before strimming or mowing.

They can get caught in garden netting, so check regularly and take netting down when it isn't needed.

You only need a few pellets, placed under a flat stone or slate with gaps for the slugs, but not hedgehogs, to get under.

Don't give them milk because it can cause diarrhoea.

Leave a pile of leaf litter and logs where hedgehogs can nest or hibernate.

How did you do?

Group sentences from the previous sheet into three paragraphs for an information text.

Paragraph 1 – Feeding hedgehogs

_____

_____

_____

Paragraph 2 – Hibernation

_____

_____

_____

Paragraph 3 – Keeping hedgehogs safe

_____

_____

_____

How did you do?

Planning paragraphs

Plan a report about children in a time you have learned about in history lessons.

Write notes for each paragraph.

Heading
Paragraph 1 – Introduction: Where and when they lived
Paragraph 2 – Homes
Paragraph 3 – Clothes
Paragraph 4 – Everyday life

How did you do?

Joke punctuation

Add punctuation marks to the jokes.

1. What happened to the boy who slept with his head under the pillow
The fairies came and took all his teeth and left £5

Use ! or ?

2. What do you get if you pour hot water down
a rabbit hole Hot cross bunnies

3. Why did the man stop his children going near
chickens Because of their fowl language

4. What's the difference between a dog and a flea
A dog can have fleas but a flea can't have dogs

5. What sits at the bottom of the sea and shivers
A nervous wreck

6. What do cats eat for breakfast
Mice crispies

7. What do you get when you cross a sheep
with a kangaroo
A woolly jumper with a pocket

How did you do?

Perfect punctuation

Use . , or ?

Add the missing punctuation marks and capital letters to the story.

'The Bundle of Sticks'
from The Fables of Aesop

there was once a man whose sons were always quarrelling they were like enemies whatever he said to them did no good at all what could he do to show them how harmful this quarrelling might be

one day the quarrelling had been much more violent than usual all the man's sons were very bad tempered he had had enough he collected a small bundle of sticks tied it with string handed it to each son in turn and told them to try to break it each one tried his hardest but couldn't break it

the man untied the bundle separated the sticks gave them to his sons and asked them to break them one by one they did this very easily

then the man told them that they were like the bundle of sticks if they helped one another any enemies would find it hard to harm them he asked what they thought would happen if an enemy attacked them when they were always quarrelling

they could see that they would be no stronger than a single stick in the bundle

although Aesop lived more than 2000 years ago his stories still have meaning today

How did you do?

Apostrophe sense

Circle incorrect apostrophes or places where apostrophes are missing. Write the words correctly.

	Corrected words
1. A polar bears favourite lunch is ice burger's.	
2. Ghosts' get through locked door's with skeleton key's.	
3. The two ghost's favourite food's were ghoulash and ice scream.	
4. Bird's fly south in winter because its' too far to walk.	
5. Heres a tip if your next holiday's in Canada: to stop a skunk smelling, hold it's nose.	
6. Its not true that cow's in Antarctica make ice cream and that's not just because there arent any cow's in Antarctica.	
7. The inventor has'nt invented anything since his waterproof teabag's and non-stick glue didn't catch on.	
8. Robin Hood didnt rob the poor because they would'nt have had anything worth stealing.	
9. If youre wondering whats bigger than an elephant but weigh's nothing, its an elephants' shadow!	

How did you do?

Knock knock inverted commas

Add inverted commas to the beginning and end of each set of spoken words.

How did you do?

Missing inverted commas

Inverted commas come at the beginning and end of what someone says.

Add the missing inverted commas.

1. Sarah, can you give me a sentence using one word 'depend'? asked the teacher.

   If you can't swim don't jump in the deep end, answered Sarah.

2. Try this one, said the teacher. Give me a sentence that includes 'benign'.

   I'm eight but I'll soon be nine, said Sarah.

3. The teacher asked his class, What's a widow?

   It's part of a wall made of glass, answered Jason.

   No. That's a window, replied the teacher and asked Jason to try again.

   I don't know, answered Jason.

   Well, what would my wife be if I died? asked the teacher.

   Sad, sir, answered Jason.

4. Another teacher asked her class, What is a parasite?

   Someone who lives in Paris, said Andrew.

5. Miss Grey asked, What do we call someone who lives in Moscow, Emma?

   Emma replied, A mosquito.

6. Now, tell me when you use inverted commas, Hayley, said the teacher

   during an English lesson.

   When I'm writing upside-down, replied Hayley.

How did you do?

Writing speech

Change these sentences so that they begin with the spoken words.

For example:

Ella said, "I'd like a glass of water, please."

"I'd like a glass of water, please," said Ella.

1. Deepak asked James, "How many legs does a centipede have?"

_____

2. James answered, "They have 100 legs. Cent means hundred."

_____

3. Deepak replied, "No! Most of them have 42 legs, but some have more than 100."

_____

4. Clare said, "Did you know that fireflies are not flies and glow worms are not worms?"

_____

5. Olivia asked, "What are they?"

_____

6. Clare answered, "Both fireflies and glow worms are beetles!"

_____

How did you do?

Correct it

Circle the punctuation mistakes in these sentences.

Write the sentences correctly.

1. "There are two punctuation mistakes in this sentence", said Amandas teacher.

_____

2. Amanda could'nt spot the mistakes, so she asked one of her friends' to help.

_____

3. "Thats it! said Nina, pointing to a mistake.

_____

4. They corrected the sentence put their books away and tidied up their classes paints.

_____

5. Their teacher said "Thank you, Amanda and Nina".

_____

6. Then the teacher asked the class to get their maths books a ruler and a sharp pencil.

_____

7. "See if you can draw a line exactly 24 millimetres long" said their teacher.

_____

How did you do?

Punctuation program

A computer's keyboard has been taken over by a bug. It writes and sends its own emails but it misses out capital letters and punctuation marks.

Put in all the missing capital letters and punctuation marks. Use a colour that will show up well.

Hi

Im hoping someone can help me Ive lost some very useful punctuation marks the first is a full stop it's just a small dot but i've heard teachers saying to children use these its amazing how they make sense of your writing

two other useful marks are the exclamation mark and the question mark the exclamation mark looks like a vertical line with a dot below it children like these so much that the one on my keyboard got worn out they can be used to show surprise or something funny such as a joke question marks look like hooks with dots below them we use them after a question they come in handy in jokes too

the next is a comma this is like a dot with a little tail most children dont bother with these but their teachers love them and i heard one this morning saying that a sentence could have two different meanings so put a comma in the right place to give it the meaning you want

lately the teacher in this class wants inverted commas all over the place if you can show me where to put these i could do it for you and keep your teacher happy

your friendly computer

How did you do?

Punctuation programmer

Write a reply to the computer's email about its lost punctuation marks.
Explain how to use each one.

Punctuation can make sense out of nonsense.

If a sentence has two possible meanings check the punctuation.

To:	From:	SEND

_____

_____

_____

_____

_____

_____

_____

How did you do?

Dialogue

A cat and a dog are discussing why they make the better type of pet. Continue their conversation using the correct punctuation to show speech. You could act it out with a friend first.

A dog is a better pet than a cat because its owner can take it for walks.

A cat can take itself for walks.

The dog said to the cat _____

_____

_____

_____

_____

_____

_____

How did you do?

Comma practice

Add commas to these sentences.

1. He bought a pineapple three cakes a packet of biscuits and some teabags.

2. During our car survey we recorded ten white cars eight black ones three red ones a silver one and a blue one.

3. At the village fair there was a bouncy castle a face-painting stall a toy stall and a sweet stall.

4. Bees flies ants ladybirds and beetles are all insects.

5. In the shop I could see a woman carrying a baby and a police officer.

6. We saw a car racing past containing three people and a bus.

7. We bought some socks and a bone for our dog.

8. "Shall we eat Mum?" asked Alice.

9. The injured dog didn't die thankfully.

10. Most of the time travellers are waiting for their luggage.

11. No one saw the burglar stealing the tablet and granddad and grandma wondered what was going on.

12. He spoke to his parents Jim and Kay and the head teacher.

How did you do?

Helpful commas

These sentences have adverbials placed before verbs.

Underline the adverbials.

Where it helps, add commas after the adverbials.

1. Every now and again I buy a comic.

2. For the last time I'm asking you to hurry.

3. At the top of the hill there was a fort.

4. To begin with I was scared of riding a two-wheeler bike.

5. For 600 years his family has lived in this castle.

6. At each side of the road they planted a long line of plane trees.

7. At long last we can get home from our holiday.

8. In snowy weather this road is closed.

9. In a flash the dog grabbed the sausage I dropped.

10. In two days' time it will be the end of term.

11. Here and there we saw a cottage on the moor.

12. Little by little the climber inched her way up the cliff.

13. As a surprise I baked a cake for my mum.

14. With a cheerful smile the boy ran to meet
    his grandparents as they came through the airport gate.

How did you do?

Sentence switch

Remember to put a comma where it is needed.

Look for the adverbials in these sentences.

Rewrite the sentences with the adverbials in front of the verbs.

1. There was a spaceship in front of our house this morning.

_____

2. It came to earth and landed in the middle of the night.

_____

3. We didn't hear a sound strangely enough.

_____

4. We could see three aliens inside the spaceship.

_____

5. We could tell they were aliens because of their green faces.

_____

6. Mum couldn't get her car out of the garage because of the spaceship.

_____

7. We had to walk to school as a result.

_____

8. The teacher listened to the story with growing amazement.

_____

How did you do?

Repair the punctuation

Add capital letters and punctuation marks to this passage.

Nurserytown Chronicle

Monday
January 27

Armed forces try to repair broken egg

on the afternoon of 6th June a large egg fell off a wall the surprising thing about this was that the kings entire cavalry was sent to repair it with an array of medical equipment the cavalry men set to work major mark tall of the kings cavalry held a short press conference at the scene in a hushed tone he explained that this was no ordinary egg and was protected by royal command it even has a name he said in a whisper he said his name is humpty dumpty

a local farmer said his sheep had names but that didn't stop people eating them as lamb chops food is food he said in a reasonable way we look after our animals during their lives but we keep them for food

another pointed out that eggs are not yet animals and even vegetarians eat them

before long it was clear that the egg couldn't be fixed with great care the cavalrymen put all the pieces in a box

a local woman who asked not to be named said

I could have made an omelette big enough for my 50 children with that egg but what did they do they put a cordon round it and wouldn't let us near

yes said another local woman mrs hubbard my cupboard was completely empty I didn't even have a bone for my dog that big egg has been wasted

How did you do?

In the news

Write your own version of the story of a nursery rhyme as a news report. Add a headline. Here are a few examples.

Little Miss Muffet	Little Bo Peep	Old Mother Hubbard	Ding Dong Bell
Girl attacked by poisonous spider	Sheep rustlers swoop on local farm	RSPCA take away woman's dog	Hero saves cat from cruel attack

Use at least two adverbials and these . ! ? , " " punctuation marks.

Nurserytown
Chronicle

Monday January 27

How did you do?

What have you learned?

Underline each clause. Circle the conjunctions that link the clauses.

I wore a sunhat and cream so that I wouldn't get burned but I forgot to put cream on my nose.

Rewrite the following, using apostrophes to show possession.

the house of the Joneses _____

a club for boys _____

the antlers belonging to two deer _____

Rewrite these using possessive pronouns, and pronouns instead of nouns.

The pen belongs to you.   The pen is _____.

The car belongs to him.   The car is _____.

The house belongs to Jim and Ann.   The house is _____.

Rewrite this using inverted commas to show what the people said.

Leah said that she had bought a present for me. I thanked her.

_____

Add an adverbial to the sentence.

We played football _____

How did you do?

Progress chart

Colour in Ollie when you have completed the chapter.

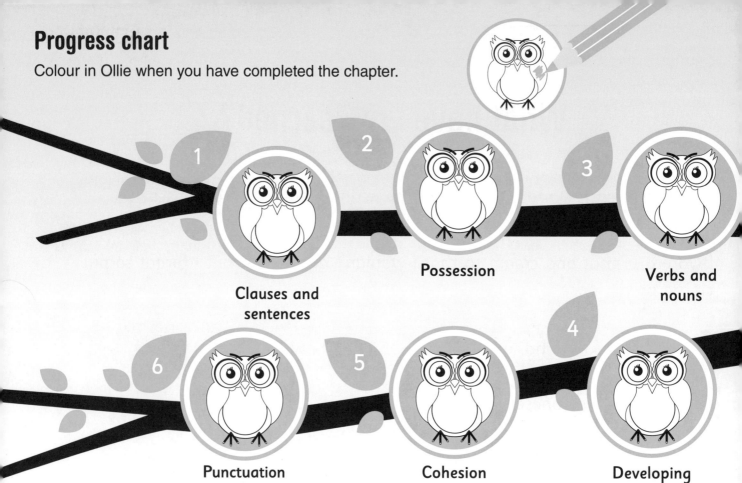

1 Clauses and sentences

2 Possession

3 Verbs and nouns

6 Punctuation

5 Cohesion

4 Developing sentences

✂ -

CONGRATULATIONS!

Name: ....

You have completed the

Grammar and punctuation **Workbook**

AGES 8–9

Age: ....   **Date:** ....